The Place Where the Sun Was

three poems
by Carolyn Collette Gray

© 2014 by Carolyn Collette Gray

All rights reserved. This book or any portion thereof may not be reproduced or used in any manner whatsoever without the express written permission of the author/publisher except for the use of brief quotations. Contact information may be found at: www.carolyncollettegray.com

Book design and cover illustration *Autumn, Filtered* by the author

First printing, 2014

ISBN-13: 978-0-9884705-1-4
ISBN-10: 0-9884705-1-9

"Dosis" font by Pablo Impallari
SIL Open Font License 1.1

to Georgia Green,
friend and mentor,
confidante and creative ally

Contents

Dedication

1. Loose Fictions — *7*
2. Fated to Dream — *23*
3. The Place Where the Sun Was — *39*

   Afterword — *57*

   About the Author — *61*

   Acknowledgements — *63*

   Index of First Lines — *65*

1. Loose Fictions

the exhalations

of living things

mingle,

saturate the atmosphere,

sustain it

i.
___

sketches for a

down-reaching dream:

children singing,

        Angels watching over me,

soldiers

making angels in the snow

it's christmas

and the world is at war

        (birds fly up in slow numbers)

ii.

daylight,
silent streets

seething waves of cold and heat,
alternating freely

ancient images in carved relief:

birds in flight
across a sky of stone

animals in human shape

a people,
lost to the ages

timeless highways in a vast frontier,
or footprints in a shifting sand

                    (thunder in a sunlit sky)

cold and beautiful ocean
thunders in the distance,
yet reaches our ears
in the merest whisper

iii.

ten thousand faces

adorn the gallery walls

each of them is you

and

one of them is me

iv.

two lives

entwined beyond the end of time

two arms

stretched out to the sky,

enthralled in a single longing

           (slow and insensible degrees

               in a great lapse of ages)

do you remember

anything of our time together?

i never saw your pain

until it was too late

and you,

you never found a way

through my hatred

that's what you started to say

when at last we gave it up,

said goodnight

although we really meant goodbye

V.

i remember red sun,

riding low as evening approached,

and the road,

beginning to bend again

after miles of straight travel

over desert,

taking on the glow of dusk

                (blood running, fever)

      Are we there yet?

      Easy now

               (another wet soul

                    enters, crying)

i remember red earth,

upturned,

low hills and a little stream

                  (a keychain, lost in tall grass)

i remember cool solitude

of rooms within rooms,

corners worn smooth,

fitted and familiar

        (a hiding game we always played)

i remember lying with you

in dusk and soft moonlight,

quietly suffused,

like twins imbued

in the womb of the universe

i remember a child

filled with silence,

stripped of joy and

robbed of promise,

all the sadness of the world

welling up inside

        (secrets to steal a life away)

and i remember waiting,

always waiting,

a dryad dream

of dusk under trees

and secret breathing,

crouching, perhaps kneeling,

a whispered benediction

of the names

of every

living

thing

                (cool gleam of evening,

                    seething with our grief)

vi.

    our time here is brief,

    prayerful, meaningless

    and utterly real

vii.

picture it:

mythic figures

from a past we never shared

                (all these worlds we never saw)

spurned in love, they

craft soliloquies

and grand deceits,

all the loose fictions

we receive

                (voices, thick with crying)

now time rolls to her slow summit

and tumbles

into careless, sobbing laughter,

happy shrieking,

sweet ragged breathing

                (a chorus of angels

                  or one, thin scream

                    on a quickening breeze)

the world is coming to an end,

its end is our beginning

drenched and ready

once again

i was blind

until i looked at you

flesh and blood,

until i touched you

grateful for the

way you change me

2. Fated To Dream

beauty reels

through this bruising world,

vast and bleeding

i.
---

fated to dream, yet never to sleep,

fevered and reeling

in the long crawl toward dawn

or half-alive in the twilight

and dying for the sun to rise

you were born

in the first electric flood

with a billion years of history,

careful, nucleic chemistry,

to be set free

of the stars, the lesser suns,

and the intervening dust

is it lonely?

is it sad?

        The darkness and the horror,

        it's more than i can bear

ii.

you were a wet soul,
afterbirth all around you

you were a new creation
grown suddenly strange,
somehow changed,
something other
than the self you'd meant to be

        (crouched and hiding,
           breathless and aware)

a time to come alive?

slip out from the shadow now,
the trees, the rain,
all covered with night, and glowing

        (fall of bare feet on pavement,
          chilled with dew beneath a
          streetlight's spill)

each moment in time

is stitched in silk thread,

                (rustle of dress,

                     trickle of mist on pale skin,

                     soft breezes sighing)

a season for being,

however brief or fleeting

iii.

but didn't you know?
the rain in this house
is always falling

little ones wonder
to be born here

iv.

sexless, free, and unreal,

she

put on her deathface

and

slipped down her doorway,

all

surreptitious, smiling

        Like i'm

        dreaming, she said

                (smoke of breath on cold air)

and

breathing again,

went

on down her street,

the

crackle of sand

beneath her tip-toe feet

V.

one kiss:

soft lips yield, and meet

for the briefest of instants

                      (eyes, luminous with dusk)

rough, hard hand on skin,

the soft skin,

sweet and gleaming in the

halogen haze

dare disturb this?

                      (shallow breathing)

        Baby, this time i mean it

one moment, like any other,

to linger over then leave behind

bid this world goodbye

        Save me

I'll let you

rapt promises, aborted courtships,
a congress of confused resolutions:

one more day
in the diary of the senses,

one more pilgrim for the ritual fire

vi.

cool and silent mystery,

occasion for joy,

                (rigid smile, searing eyes)

you be a killer and

i'll be a boy,

you be a sunset

and i'll be the west,

you be a lover,

i'll be love's

last

breath

vii.

basic, animal
big-top death games

high-wire suicides and
new dimensions
in desperate chances

meaningful glances,
unmistakable birth trances

carnival walking,
speakers talking,
places without names

a community of ruined faces,
of dreams worn like traces
of yesterday's makeup

voices, threatening to break up
over each lost chord
in this awful song

        Help me in this song,
        come along

viii.

a saxophone plays
in a city under summer dusk

shimmer of rooftops, streets,
mirroring the distance,
relinquishing their heat

                    (music, laughter, shouting)

lovers grin, children sin,
discover it's delicious,
dangerous and real

all in a day and it's all okay:
we can live out our lives in the sun
and die, so glad to be released
and young

tell the children

our dead fly up to heaven,

pale flowers, like souls,

rooted to soil

in which they cannot grow

3. The Place Where the Sun Was

we shape the very

air we breathe

and

call it Speech

i.
---

within

rising crescendos of pain

and

not especially christ-like
in demeanor,

we're gonna live like kings
and die like gods

yeah, it's gonna be epic

ii.

frogs,

rushes

cool nights in shallow marshes

vital slime

moon in sky, wind in trees,
a gentle breeze

a murmur:

of life?

                    (arousal, rising)

two lovers,
entwined in desire

one is Nature, the other
only Reason, dressed in rags

says,

          Are ya glad ta see me?

she sighs,

drops her eyes and

smiles,

holds him like a child

whispers,

       Goodbye

iii.

her eyes close and she smiles,

thinks to herself, it's

been a while

since anybody cared to ask,

it's been a while since she last

closed her eyes and smiled

iv.

storm is coming

smell of rain, sound of thunder
in the distance

a flicker
or a flash of light,
searching out across the sky

insect Night,
split for an instant

a still life in black and white

V.

you sent your invitations
word of mouth, shouted
down hallways, telephones,
lunched-over, hand-delivered

under stars and wet clouds,
beneath trees and
'round back of sheds, woodpiles,

you sought your guests' affection,
friends' attention,
a name, or a place

burned fingers and fire,
sweating pitchers and
someone's drugs upstairs,

smiles ignited
in the glow of pure communion
moved you to tears,
to completeness and confusion

and now, with goodbyes
whispered to a special few,
crooned loosely in tune with
tires down the driveway,

you linger out and count
around your feet some moths,
dropping from the
streetlight's warmth
down to the pavement
with the rain

vi.

wild, impetuous life itself,

i

slit my wrists to witness you

speak your name to summon you,

fly out across the universe

and lose you

wish to be with you,

so glad to see you

but where in all this dark

am i supposed to find you,

when there's so little reason to believe

we've ever even been apart

or

might someday come to be ?

vii.

fatal rapture

brief incandescence,
iridescence,
then a long, slow fade

comes the sun?

a city rises from the dust,
angry in its grief
already

always and again

forever

viii.

by morning,

rain has turned the sun

to blood

and we are young again

ix.

air all gilt, or bronzed,

a sweet intermingling

of sunrise and soft leaf-fall

brief mystery,

or the memory of heartache

                (touched,

                      not a word spoken)

in the dream

we see you walking,

slowly and

without apparent purpose

knife in your hand

shines from the light

that surrounds you

a shiver

seems to shake you,

makes you slash the air

and speak a word

we can't quite understand

        (lovingly:)

    Somehow we knew

    you would come to this,

    pale flower,

    The place where the sun was

in the dream,

i'm trying to reach you,

but you

can't seem to see me at all

Afterword

What's the word I'm looking for?

It has to do with the notion of Deep Time, I think. Of the immensity of — what? years? centuries? eons? — flowing out behind us. Possibly not to infinity, but so distant as to defy imagination, exceed the capability of our mental wiring, surpass the reach of our instinct or intuition.

It has to do with Right Now as well, this word I'm looking for: the single slice of time we call the Moment in which we live. A slice of which can be further divided, of course, in half then half again and so on toward another unreachable infinity, in theory at least. A paradox in measurement, of the sort that Zeno describes.

And it has to do with Nostalgia, the wistful longing for someone or something receding irrevocably to the horizon behind us. But transpose this nostalgia, in a way, so that it describes the phenomenon even as we experience the event, even as it happens. Before it all begins to slip away into what we call our histories.

And slip away it will — it does — trailing out after us slow or fast, near or far, depending on our perception as the process unfolds. Unstoppable. Irretrievable.

Transpose it all so that the smile of remembrance, the fondness of recollection — and, yes, the pang of loss and regret — so that it all begins to seep in at the very instant we experience or observe. So that every experience, every observation, becomes at once a memory that will dwell in the past far, far longer than it ever persisted in the present. As real and true then as now.

What's the word I'm looking for? Is there any human language that completely, concisely describes this? Or is it like a color in an endlessly subtle spectrum, easily seen yet somehow unnamed in any catalog of what our senses take in?

What's it called?

In French, we might look to the entries alongside *déjà vu* — *déjà disparu*, perhaps, the sense that everything has always already been gone? In German, we could string a series of words together, meld a collection of concepts into a single, long, imperfectly blended amalgam representing an idea.

In English, it may be that there is no single word. Maybe the best we can do is struggle or strive to explain the sensation not in one utterance but in sentences, paragraphs, whole conversations. A dialog, extending without arbitrary limit out ahead of us, into the future.

Out, at least, until we've satisfied the need, the primal desire, to connect. To tell another, *This is what I feel, this is who I am* — and to know that we've been heard. To know that another understands, a little bit. Has glimpsed, at least for an instant, this Life as we ourselves live it, as we see it, as it appears to our own eyes.

And to realize that, in so doing, they've made this Life, this World, this near-infinity of Experiences, a little less lonely for us both. If only for a moment.

About the Author

Carolyn Collette Gray lives and writes on the seacoast in New England. In this edition, she presents three short works on the seeming timelessness of relationships, the distances that grow between ourselves and the ones we love, and the sense of nostalgia that sometimes tempers our experiences even as events occur.

www.carolyncollettegray.com

Acknowledgements

As sharp-eyed readers will have noticed, my use in *Loose Fictions* of the phrase "slow and insensible degrees in a great lapse of ages" is paraphrased from Charles Lyell's *Principles of Geology*, which he published in 1833. Now there's someone who knew a little bit about deep time and the unfathomable passage of years.

Index of First Lines

a saxophone plays — 36

air all gilt, or bronzed — 53

basic, animal — 35

beauty reels — 25

but didn't you know? — 30

by morning — 52

cool and silent mystery — 34

daylight (silent streets) — 12

fatal rapture — 51

fated to dream, yet never to sleep — 27

frogs (rushes) — 44

her eyes close and she smiles — 46

i remember red sun — 15

i was blind (until i looked at you) — 21

in the dream — 55

one kiss (soft lips yield) — 32

our time here is brief — 18

picture it (mythic figures) — 19

sexless, free, and unreal — 31

sketches (for a down-reaching dream) — 11

storm is coming — 47

tell the children — 37

ten thousand faces — 13

the exhalations (of living things) — 9

two lives (entwined) — 14

we shape (the very air) — 41

wild, impetuous (life itself) — 50

within (rising crescendos of pain) — 43

you sent your invitations — 48

you were a wet soul — 28

www.ingramcontent.com/pod-product-compliance
Lightning Source LLC
Chambersburg PA
CBHW070633050426
42450CB00011B/3172